FOUNDATIONS OF ORDER

*Understanding The Need
for Biblical
Church Government
in The Last Days*

**Local Church Government Series
Volume I**

by

Dr. Lawrence Kennedy

**The North Church
Carrollton, Texas**

Copyrights and Permissions

Unless otherwise indicated, all Scripture quotations are taken from THE NEW KING JAMES VERSION of the Bible. Copyright © 1982, Thomas Nelson, Inc. All rights reserved.

Scripture quotations marked (Ampl.) are taken from THE AMPLIFIED NEW TESTAMENT copyright © 1958, 1987 by The Lockman Foundation. Used by permission.

Scripture quotations marked (NAS) are taken from THE NEW AMERICAN STANDARD BIBLE © Copyright The Lockman Foundation 1960, 1962, 1963, 1968, 1971, 1972, 1973, 1975, 1977, 1988. Used by permission.

Scripture quotations marked (KJV) are taken from THE KING JAMES VERSION of the Bible.

References marked (Strong's # # # #) are taken from the Strong's Electronic Concordance (KJV). Copyright © 1989 TriStar Publishing. All rights reserved. Used by permission.

Statistics referenced in text are courtesy of *The Barna Report*, Barna Research Group. Oxnard, California.

Copyright © 1997 by Houghton Mifflin Company. Adapted and reproduced by permission from The American Heritage College Dictionary, Third Edition.

Permission to quote Dr. Bob Mason, Founder and President, Missions International—Chiapas Expedition, was expressly granted by Dr. Mason.

Local Church Government Series: Volume I
Foundations of Order:
Understanding The Need for Biblical Church Government in The Last Days
Copyright © 1998 by Dr. Lawrence Kennedy

Published by The North Church
1615 West Belt Line Road
Carrollton, Texas 75006

International Standard Book Number 0-9663308-0-3

Library of Congress Catalog Card Number: 98-65266

All rights reserved under International Copyright Law. No portion of this book may be used or reproduced in whole or in part in any form without the written permission of the publisher.

Printed in the United States of America.

*I dedicate this book and series to the Body of Christ
and to local churches throughout America and the world.
To my wife and partner in ministry, Coral,
and to the congregation of the North Church—without
your love, prayerful support and faithfulness
to the Lord's calling on your lives,
this book could not have been written.*

TABLE OF CONTENTS

INTRODUCTION vi

CHAPTER 1
The Call To Order *1*

    Decently & In Order
    For An Eternal Purpose

CHAPTER 2
Order Versus Chaos...*5*

    The Need For Order
    The Origin Of The Universe
    Making Sense Out of Nonsense
    Summing It Up

CHAPTER 3
The Importance of The Word of God..*13*

    HIS-story Is His Blueprint
    The Call of Wisdom
    Proper Study of God's Word
    Illumination of Heart And Spirit
    We Must Move Together

CHAPTER 4
God's Progressive Revelation..*23*

    From The Old . . . To The New
    The Adopted
    Spiritual Jerusalem
    The Temple of God
    The Bride of Christ
    Summing It Up

CHAPTER 5
The Kingdom And The Church..*35*

    Earthly Kingdoms
    The Sure Foundation
    God's Kingdom Order
    Summing It Up
    Kingdom Order And The Church
    The Mystical And The Concrete
    The Church Throughout The Ages

CHAPTER 6
Biblical Principles of Spiritual Growth And Order 57

    Living Unto The Lord
    Completing One Another in Love
    Fulfilling The Law of Christ
    Walking Softly With God
    A Word To Pastors
    A Word To God's People

CONCLUSION
The Final Word 67

INTRODUCTION

For the past 27 years, I have studied biblical patterns of order within the local church and counseled with church leaders around the world. During this time, I have found several things to be true. Healthy local churches that operate according to God's established order bring life and vitality to their people and communities. Churches that lack a biblical government structure often struggle just to survive and experience heartbreaking results. Many churches and people with great potentials for God have been hindered because they lacked understanding of the foundations of order in the Christian life. It is for this reason I am writing this minibook; the first of several volumes in a series about Local Church Government.

Healthy local churches are vital, living and breathing, spiritual organisms (Ephesians 4:1-16 & Romans 12:4-5). They are the foundation stones for healthy lives. Jesus said to Peter in Matthew 16:18, *" . . . on this rock I will build My church, and the gates of Hades shall not prevail against it."* God has a plan for His people to function in proper order; a detailed blueprint for us to follow in the pages of the Bible. The book of 2 Peter 2:9-10 contains an eye-opening statement, *"the Lord knows how to deliver the godly out of temptations and to reserve the unjust under punishment for the day of judgment, and especially those who walk according to the flesh in the lust of uncleanness and despise authority [government, KJV] . . ."*

It is *critical* for every Christian to be added by God to a local body of believers where they can learn to submit to God's delegated authorities and grow in His spiritual Kingdom. Likewise, it is the responsibility of pastors to teach their congregations what the Bible says about God's Kingdom and Church—and lead them in applying this knowledge to everyday life.

Christians must know the origins of what they believe; they must know their spiritual roots. Every child of God needs to understand who they are in Christ and their function within God's family. We should also know how God's family operates within His Kingdom realm. Those that do not often fall by the wayside of Christianity and never fulfill their God-given destinies. *This breaks God's heart.* It is also a sad fact that many wounded believers unknowingly hurt others—which hinders the Body of Christ *and* God's purpose to spread the Gospel to the ends of the earth.

There cannot be a glorious Church without glorious saints! This is why I have chosen to address the human element first in this series. (The subsequent mini-books will focus on specific areas of local church government.) In this volume, I discuss humanity's basic need for order and how it can be found in the Bible—our blueprint for living. I talk about perception, and how if Christians are not careful, our understanding of God's established order can be perverted. I also look closely at the biblical foundations of the Kingdom of God and the Church, and review Scriptural principles that lay the foundations of order within every believer (and ultimately, the local church and universal Body of Christ).

This mini-book series has been designed to help you, no matter who you are, or what function you perform within the Body of Christ. Senior pastors, staff pastors, lay leaders, or church members from any denomination will benefit from reading the entire Local Church Government series.

From Genesis to Revelation, God has provided a detailed plan for establishing and growing healthy local churches and building healthy lives. I believe that as you gain a complete understanding of the foundations of order, you will begin to find the answers you seek. I pray that the Holy Spirit will give you special insight and perception of the Word of God as we search the Scriptures regarding His Kingdom and Church. And finally, I pray that as you discover the necessity for proper order within the local church, you will find and fulfill your eternal destiny.

CHAPTER 1
The Call To Order

There was once a dynamic local church that underwent a change in leadership. This church had grown to over 1,000 members in a relatively short period of time, and despite many challenges. Then at the most successful time in the church's history, the Lord called the founding pastors to another assignment.

The search for a new pastor began, and with high recommendations from many peers, he was set in place. This minister was respected and accomplished. He had been used mightily of God and the fruit of the Holy Spirit rested on his ministry. Yet, within a few years, the church had suffered a split and its membership had fallen to one third of its original size.

What happened? Are changes in leadership bad for the local church? Not necessarily. Do all churches suffer splits when the founding pastor receives another assignment from the Lord? Absolutely not! The truth is that great preaching, teaching and dynamic ministry (in and of themselves) do not provide an adequate foundation for establishing and growing a strong local church.

The church mentioned above had not grown to its maximum size simply because of great pulpit ministry. It had become dynamic and effective because a biblical church government system had originally been set in place. The members had been *"knit together"* by the Holy Spirit (Ephesians 4:16). They were operating in their God-given functions and relating properly to other members in the body.

Decently And In Order

A sound government structure based on biblical principles and led by the Holy Spirit is *critical* to the life, health and overall effectiveness of the local church. Church government was designed by God to bring order within local church bodies, according to Ephesians 4:11-12 and 1 Corinthians 14:26, 33 & 40. All things are to be done *"decently and in order."* Where there is no church government, people *and* church functions suffer. New growth is stifled and existing functions are either hampered, or they deteriorate.

King Solomon wrote in the book of Ecclesiastes that there is a time and season for everything (3:1). If Christians truly believe this Scripture, we would be very selective about the things we do for God, especially within the local church. I believe that as Christians submit themselves to the leadership of the Holy Spirit within their local church, God will make everything in their lives *"beautiful"* in His perfect timing (Ecclesiastes 3:11).

According to Ecclesiastes 3:22, a person's work is their lot in life. King Solomon—one of the wisest men to ever live on planet earth—wrote that there is nothing better than to enjoy one's work. God surely had this in mind when He created you and me, and decided what purpose we would fulfill within the local church. The gifts and passions we possess for God point the way to our purpose, and enable us to fulfill it. *There's also an added blessing.* The Christian that lives according to God's design experiences incredible peace, joy and fulfillment in life.

For An Eternal Purpose

If work is a drudgery, bringing confusion instead of peace and frustration instead of fulfillment—*it is time for you to find out if you are living within God's purpose.* How can the Church reach out to a lost and dying world if we are just as lost as they are? The blind cannot lead the blind—*not God's way*. God intends for Christians to live overcoming lives *doing* what He has created us to do. God does not send confusion, strife, or any other form of darkness into His Church. He is light. As His people, we receive His light and abundant life by knowing His plan and walking in it.

God is sounding the wake-up call. He is speaking to the end-time Church that we are to become a community of Christ; a shining example to those who are looking for and desiring something real. We are the *"salt"* and *"light"* that God has sent into the world to dispel darkness (Matthew 5:13-16). We *must* overcome so that we can offer to others the hope we have received in Jesus Christ.

The Christian's place to receive help is within the local church; a specific spiritual home where we are perfected in the faith (*remember* Ephesians 4:12-13). We should not "float around" in the world without a home! This is not God's order for Christian living. He gives each of His children a specific spiritual family on earth, within the larger Body of Christ. It is within this family unit that we receive healing and instruction, and grow within God's purpose. It is also within the local church that Christians learn to walk in unity and submit to God's delegated authorities (Hebrews 13:17).

Our ultimate authority, of course, is God. We have been bought with the priceless blood of Jesus and sealed into God's spiritual family by the Holy Spirit. God is the rightful owner of our lives and everything we possess. His purpose is greater than anyone's personal agenda, or any rights we may think we hold to our ideas, gifts and/or ministries.

Yet in return, every born-again Christian has received the promise of eternal life and the ability to live abundantly today. The devil has lost his power! The flesh is too weak to control us. God's strength is being *"made perfect"* in us (2 Corinthians 12:9). Through Jesus Christ, we have received everything we need for life and godliness (2 Peter 1:3).

Right now, the greatest revival ever known to man is being set into motion. As people see the love and unity of believers around the world, they are going to come running to the Last Day Church! People are going to hear a clear voice calling them. They are going to sense peace within the walls of the local church, and they are going to find it; because my friend, Jesus is perfecting His people and bringing His Church into proper biblical order.

CHAPTER 2
Order Versus Chaos

As a troubled boy from a dysfunctional home, I saw and experienced a great deal of needless pain and heartbreak. I wanted peace and harmony, but often fell victim to the disorder in my family and the pain that resulted from it. My desire to study and understand order was birthed from these harsh circumstances. I guess you could say I knew what didn't work, so I started looking for something that would.

Comparing my early life to the present-day Church, I have seen that many Christians desire proper order, but become victims of spiritual dysfunction and uncontrolled emotions. We try to defend our self interests instead of responding to problems in a spirit of love and sacrifice. It is painfully obvious in a local church when something is operating out of order, because everyone seems to suffer (see 1 Corinthians 12:26). Like that troubled little boy, we all know when something is not working.

Human power is unable to break the chain of reaction in human behavior. We can try to manage our emotions—but we cannot always control them. Only God can do this. He is the only one qualified to be God. I've read the job description! " *'The Spirit of the Lord is upon Me, because He has anointed Me to preach the gospel to the poor; He has sent Me to heal the brokenhearted, to proclaim liberty to the captives and recovery of sight to the blind, to set at liberty those who are oppressed; to proclaim the acceptable year of the Lord'* " (Luke 4:18-19 & Isaiah 61:1-2a).

Jesus Christ is the source of order, according to Isaiah 9:6-7a, *"For unto us a Child is born, unto us a Son is given;*

and the government will be upon His shoulder. And His name will be called Wonderful, Counselor, Mighty God, Everlasting Father, Prince of Peace. Of the increase of His government and peace there will be no end."

The Need for Order

The need for order lies deep within our hearts. This is proven by humanity's constant search for knowledge and significance. People seem to have an unquenchable thirst to understand and manipulate the vast resources that make up the known world. This thirst has existed within the soul of man since the beginning of time. In fact, it was instituted by God when He created humanity and gave us dominion over the earth and everything in it (Genesis 1:26,28). Chapter 3 of the book of Genesis records what happened when Adam and Eve took their eyes off of God; they fell into deception and sinned. Mankind lost dominion through Adam, but Romans 5:17-19 tells us that Jesus Christ paid the price to buy it back for us. He is the second Adam—our Source of order.

For the unbeliever, the need for order usually begins with a search for the answers to life's most basic questions.

- "Is there a God?"
- "How did the world begin?"
- "How did humanity originate?"
- "Why is there evil in the world?"
- "What happens when people die?"

For the believer, the answers to these questions are simple. They lie within the realm of faith. By faith, we understand how we came into being, where we will go after death, the course of humanity, and the spiritual origins of good and evil. We must also believe that God has the answers for our daily living. Let us test our hearts today, according to 1 Corinthians 11:31. Do we believe that the Lord has the answer to *every* question and the solution to *every* problem in our lives, *or do we have faith in only what we can see and experience through our natural senses?*

Living by faith is a foundational principle of the Kingdom of God, as well as within the local church. God is our ultimate authority and the author of order. In His Word, He has outlined principles of order that every believer must follow to live a happy and successful life. Jesus walked in complete submission to the Father while He lived on the earth. This required a great deal of faith, *especially* when He walked toward certain death on the Cross. In kind, we must submit to our spiritual authorities in a humble attitude of faith toward God.

Just as a person receives Jesus Christ as their Savior by faith, he must exercise faith to live and function within the Body of Christ and the local church. As a believer trusts in the existence of God and His creation of the universe, she must trust Him to live within His divine plan *right now*. Just as a person is assured of going to heaven, he or she must understand that God has a special place and function for them on earth. It is as simple as that.

Faith is a gift from God. Once given, it becomes a choice; an act of the will. You see, everyone believes in *something*. What you and I have faith in is made obvious each day by what we choose to say and do. As believers in Christ, we must *choose* to set aside our self-interests to cooperate with others in a spirit of love and unity. Christians from every walk of life must learn to rise above our natural senses and exercise *absolute faith* in God and His unchanging Word.

The book of Ecclesiastes 3:11 also tells us that God has placed *"eternity"* in the heart of man. *Jesus Christ, the author and finisher of your faith, is the only one that can help you find the order God has placed within you* (see Hebrews 12:1-2). When Jesus quenches your thirst, you will never thirst again. *" 'If anyone thirsts, let him come to Me and drink. He who believes in Me, as the Scripture has said, out of his heart will flow rivers of living water' "* (John 7:37b-38).

The Origin of The Universe

Let us go back to the foundation of order itself, the beginning of the universe. The book of Genesis tells us that *"God created the heavens and the earth"* (1:1). God sculpted the universe using the power of His creative Word. He existed before creation, extends beyond all creation, and encompasses the fullness of His creation. God is Alpha and Omega. He brought order and life to a formless, shapeless void. Humanity's need for order is rooted in the fabric of creation—God. *There is no other.*

Earthly wisdom tries to persuade us otherwise. For example, the Big Bang theory states that the universe constantly evolves and expands until it flies apart—an endless chain of reaction. Because of this, scientists believe that the universe originated from an explosion of some type of mass. Scientists have also observed that cosmic radiation arrives at earth from every direction in space—the probable result of a big bang. They have other reasons for this theory, but one important fact is missing. *Where did the original mass come from?*

Before modern science was developed, some tried to answer life's questions by creating myths. A myth does not reflect the truth; instead, it attempts to explain things that reach beyond human senses and abilities. Greek mythology explains what existed before the known universe as Chaos—the lord of disorder. From disorder came Erebus (death) and Nix (darkness). Then somehow, out of nowhere, Eros (sensual love) came into being—which was the mythological beginning of order.

Whether we want to admit it or not, Christians can be affected by these secular theories. Science has attempted to rationalize a supernatural reality; to grasp, hold and manipulate it according to man's abilities. Ancient Greek influences continue to affect today's post-modern society. *Christians be warned!* When we see ungodly innuendoes in our communities, through the media, or in some form of art, we must *recognize* them for what they are. Subtly formed lies from the enemy. Our perception of God's Word and the truths we believe by faith can be altered by these (and other) worldly belief systems.

Making Sense Out of Nonsense

To agree with mythology, one would first have to believe that disorder, death and darkness are the foundations of the known universe. If this were true, the 3 D's would be the root ingredients of everything that exists in the world today. *This is ridiculous!* God is our creator. I can see Him in every part of creation, as well as have fellowship with Him in my spirit. His beauty can be seen in the face of a newborn baby, His glory is revealed in nature, and His presence gives peace to troubled souls. God is omniscient, omnipotent and omnipresent. *He is absolutely unlimited.* He gives truth, life and light to everything He creates.

Secondly, the idea that sensual love brings order makes no sense at all. A word study of the word "eros" reveals that this kind of love is rooted in the need for self-preservation. How could self-love bring order and balance to a universe filled with different organisms and species? A quick look at the daily news tells us that sensual love expressed outside of God's order brings heartbreak and disaster. Teenage pregnancy, sexually transmitted diseases, and broken marriages are just a few of the results of sensual love expressed out of order.

The word "agape" describes God's perfect love. Agape love blends affection and generosity with social and moral obligation. The love of God brought order to the universe and brings order and harmony to our everyday world.

Without God, there is no order. Without order, there is chaos. Chaos is confusion, and confusion always brings pain—the root of dysfunction.

Summing It Up

Secular science principles have put the reality of God's expanding universe into a neat little box. Since rational thought excludes faith, it fails to recognize that God existed *before* creation, expands *beyond* creation, and encompasses *the fullness* of creation. God is the origin of the universe and the reason why it expands beyond man's ability to measure it. We are not the results of an endless chain of reaction! *We are the fruits of a divine plan and purpose.*

Mythology would try to convince us that confusion, death and darkness give birth to life. *Tell me, has this been your experience?* It certainly has not been mine.

As mentioned earlier, 1 Corinthians 14:40 instructs that everything in the local church must be done *"decently and in order."* This principle was powerfully demonstrated in God's creation of the universe—the heavens and the earth formed by the power of His Word. God is not the author of confusion. He brings order, beauty and balance to His entire creation. God works in and through *all* things. He works *"all things together"* for good (Romans 8:28).

God gave us the gift of His Word to bring purpose, peace and security to our lives. By exercising faith and following God's principles of order, we will no longer be prone to dysfunction and disorder—the results of living outside of God's plan. The Word of God has every answer we seek and the solution to every problem we face—individually and corporately. Everything and everyone God creates has a special purpose and place within His divine plan.

The local church is a vital element in God's plan to redeem humanity. It is the vessel through which God has chosen to manifest His presence, power and glory in the earth. As you will read in the following chapters, the church is the place where God's people are perfected in the faith and prepared to help others. It is a place of unity and harmony. Every person in the local church is an *essential part* of a healthy spiritual organism—a local family within the universal family of God. It is not God's will for anyone in the Body of Christ to stand alone, or to pursue his or her personal agenda at the expense or exclusion of others. There should be no "Lone Rangers" in God's Kingdom!

God did not intend for life to be an endless chain of reactions to problems and hurts. It is *not* God's will that His children live in confusion and pain. God's purpose is that we obey the counsel of His Word and become everything He has created us to be . . . a *united* family that has been called to be *vital* and *effective* for the glory of God.

CHAPTER 3
The Importance of The Word of God

To operate within God's plan of order, we must first understand what His order is. We must understand the Bible. Nationwide surveys conducted by The Barna Group have revealed that Bible reading in America has reached dangerously low levels; less than 40% of Americans read the Bible weekly. Slightly more than 50% of society actually believes the Bible is literal truth. . . . *And* even though most American households own several Bibles, people spend less than one-half percent of their week reading even *one* of them! It is no wonder that people are fighting among themselves, and so many Christians are having serious problems doing what is right before God. We must understand in practical terms the importance of the Word of God and the illuminating ministry of the Holy Spirit in victorious Christian living.

The Bible is preeminent. This means the truths it contains are far superior to earthly wisdom. They are eternal; not limited by time, space, or opinion. The Bible is God's creative Word revealed to men, a *living* record of His heavenly wisdom. It imparts life to everyone that reads and obeys its principles. God's Word facilitates spiritual growth and success in every area that is submitted to its influence. God said through the prophet Isaiah—

> *"For as the heavens are higher than the earth, so are My ways higher than your ways, and My thoughts than your thoughts. For as the rain comes down, and the snow from heaven, and do not return there, but water the earth, and make it bring forth and bud*

. . . . So shall My word be that goes forth from my mouth; it shall not return to Me void, but it shall accomplish what I please, and it shall prosper in the thing for which I sent it" (55:9-10).

Like the rain and snow that give life to everything on the earth, the Bible imparts life to every believer. We need the life-giving Word of God in order to live the overcoming, abundant lives He has for us! *You cannot achieve your eternal destiny by using your own strength, abilities, or intellect.* Supernatural strength, ability and insight are released to God's people as His Word waters our lives, and causes us to grow and flourish.

To deny the importance of the Word of God is to commit spiritual suicide. *It is insane!* I often tell my congregation that *"insanity is doing the same thing over and over again, expecting a different result."* Let me say that choosing to ignore the Bible and follow our earthly wisdom—where we are prone to making shortsighted decisions over and over again—is insanity. God's wisdom is superior! Let's get smart, and do things God's way.

HIS-story Is His Blueprint

The Bible is literal history; a blueprint of past, present and future. Its authenticity is proven by geographical, historical and archaeological records. The Bible records the rich heritage of the nation of Israel (and others) through many generations, even beyond the existence of man. Its accuracy is also proven by the events taking place today in Israel. It's amazing. Nations of far greater size and scope than this tiny nation are totally dependent upon her well being. Israel has confounded the top minds of this age; and many scholars have admitted that they have merely scratched the surface of the magnificent, yet simple, truths contained in the Bible.

I like to call the Word of God, *HIS-story*. It is the ordered text of the Alpha-Omega, a comprehensive eternal plan.

Thousands of years of human history fall in and between the pages of the Bible. When we study the Word with a systematic approach, we get a much clearer picture of where we came from and where we are going. It is what I call having *eternal vision:* seeing life from a bird's-eye view, perceiving every dimension, and through the eyes of faith . . . gaining a greater understanding of life than ever before.

God's vision is proactive and retroactive. He sees every angle. You see, when God looks at something, it is as though He's viewing a movie. He produced it, He directed it, and then He plays it back to us. We become characters in the cast that are living out His purpose on the earth. Every believer has their own personality and their own way of reading His script and performing, but the Bible gives the plot, theme and purpose—*the true meaning of life*.

Through studying the Bible, we gain supernatural understanding, security and peace in knowing there is a Mastermind that is weaving the threads of a brilliant, eternal plan. Human history is at the heart of its purpose. This same merciful Genius decided thousands of years ago to write a living testimony that would empower you and me to run the race set before us with hope and endurance. The book of Habbakuk 2:2-3 says,

" . . . Write the vision and make it plain upon tablets, that he may run who reads it. For the vision is yet for an appointed time; but at the end it will speak, and it will not lie. Though it tarries, wait for it; because it will surely come, it will not tarry."

Unlike best-selling books written by some of the most prominent minds in the world, the Bible was penned by the only One that is not limited by the physical realm. God will never suffer from disease of the mind or body, He is not controlled by emotions or opinions, and He will never die. *Do you see now why I say it is insane to not follow God?*

He is the only one qualified to be God. Only Jesus can perfect humanity and lead His people into absolute truth, strength and victory.

The Call of Wisdom

King Solomon chose the right thing—wisdom. He followed the path of wisdom and was blessed with a prosperous and productive life. The book of Proverbs 4:7 states that *"wisdom is the principal thing."* If we apply ourselves to understanding and following God's wisdom, we will reap positive results today, just as King Solomon did in the Old Testament.

God has given us the ability to learn from the victories and failures of others by studying the Bible, His book of wisdom. The Bible is very transparent; it reflects both good and evil. We can learn from the mistakes and shortcomings of people in the Bible and avoid making the same mistakes ourselves. We can also model the victories recorded in Scripture to achieve real success—living to please our heavenly Father.

When we live according to God's design, we reap God's best for our lives. Galatians 6:8 says, *"For he who sows to his flesh will of the flesh reap corruption, but he who sows to the Spirit will of the Spirit reap everlasting life."* Let us choose to set aside any distractions and invest in eternity! We must seek the counsel of God, as reflected in the Bible—our eternal instruction book. We will reap in due season if we do not lose heart in doing what is right (Galatians 6:9).

If you are in a difficult place today, there is hope! God has a specific plan for you, and this plan includes a special place and function for you within the local church. You will learn His plan by carefully reading His Word and through the illuminating ministry of the Holy Spirit. Remember, God is more brilliant than any person that has ever walked on the face of the earth. By listening to God and following His ways, you will operate from a higher IQ, and handle life better than ever before.

When God reveals your place within the local church, get to that place and get busy doing what God has created you to do! You already possess the gifts, passion and strength to fulfill His unique purpose for your life.

Make developing an intimate relationship with God your top priority for living. Your life, and the local church God has created you to be a part of, will never be the same.

Proper Study of God's Word

As children of God, we must be students of the Bible. We should understand and apply sound principles of biblical interpretation, whether we are in the ministry or not. Since not everyone can take a course in hermeneutics, I am going to briefly review a few of the basic principles of Bible study. As I do, remember 2 Timothy 2:15, *"Study and be eager and do your utmost to present yourself to God approved (tested by trial), a workman who has no cause to be ashamed, correctly analyzing and accurately dividing [rightly handling and skillfully teaching] the Word of Truth"* (Ampl.).

Every one of us "handles" the Word of God in one way or another. What about the busy executive who has a thousand things spinning around in his or her thoughts, and anxiety to match? What about the frazzled convenience store clerk that is up to his or her elbows in merchandise and demanding customers? There are millions of people in the world and many different situations in life. One thing is sure: we must all get a grip on the Word of God.

What about you? How do you "handle" the Word of God in your daily life? Is it easy for you to study and understand the Bible, or could you use a little help?

In interpreting the Word, I merge many theologies together. I rarely separate and label them, because God does not do this. He synthesizes. As I said before, God works all things *together* for good. In studying Scripture, we must synthesize. We must take the *literal* (or historic) meaning of Scripture, balance it with the *principle* (or moral) that is being taught, then complete the picture with the *prophetic* (or ultimate) meaning.

The *literal* meaning is very important, because it is the groundwork for spiritual revelation. There is a tendency within the Body of Christ to not study the literal aspects of scripture; the history and geography, culture and original languages. It is our duty to interpret the Bible consistent with all of these areas, and there are many ways to do so. Bible encyclopedias or atlases are excellent historical resources. Some of the more comprehensive study Bibles include a certain amount of this information. Find what works for you and use it!

Principles of the Bible are the truths that can be applied in almost any situation at any point in history. For example, even though many Old Testament traditions are no longer practiced, they provide sound standards for New Testament living. Principles provide the wisdom of practical experience. They are not to be literally interpreted. When you read the Bible, always look for the underlying principle that is being taught. The Holy Spirit can help you with this.

The *prophetic* meaning of Scripture is based on the premise that Old Testament passages have a deeper meaning by which they anticipate the New Testament Church age. It is only when the prophetic meaning is applied to Scripture that the Bible truly becomes one book. Certain books of the Bible are entirely prophetic; but be careful, prophecy can be found throughout the Word of God!

Some key questions to ask yourself when you read prophetic passages include, *1) How does this relate to Jewish people and their literal and natural circumstances?, 2) How does it apply to the Church and end-time events?,* and *3) How can Christians apply it to their daily lives?* You will not have to read prophecy for very long before you discover that the

Church age and Messianic prophecies are blended into Old Testament history like the spirit is blended with body and soul.

Illumination of Heart And Spirit

Finally, let me say that God has so designed Scripture that our understanding of it is weaved into our hearts, as well as in our intellects. To comprehend the Bible, we must balance the subjective with the objective. For example, we cannot discount the fact that natural Israel is an important part of our spiritual heritage. If we do, we are in trouble. Yet, we must *walk out* our faith in Jesus Christ as joint-heirs with every right, privilege and responsibility of God's natural children. If we do not, we are headed for trouble. We must read the Bible and live according to its principles.

Our personal spiritual experience has a profound affect on our understanding of God's Word. If we walk what we talk, the Word is literally *"made flesh"* in our lives. It is a lamp to our feet and a light to our paths (Psalm 119:105). If a person's walk does not match his or her talk, then the Bible becomes hard to read and even more difficult to understand. Some people have closed its pages permanently because the Bible removes them from their shaded place of comfort. Believe me, this oasis is an illusion; and without the grace of God, it is a place of no return.

In biblical times, Christ spoke in parables to veil the truth from those whose hearts were closed and ears were dull (Matthew 13:10-15). It doesn't have to be that way with us! We are Jesus' spiritual offspring . . . His heirs. His friends (John 15:15). If we seek and obey Him, making the Word of God the top priority in our everyday lives, there will be nothing hidden from us. We will know our God and stand in the light of His Word, purpose and power.

We Must Move Together

The book of Numbers 13 & 14:20-38 record how a generation of faithless Israelites received a life sentence in the wilderness because they did not obey the Word of the Lord. They were focused on themselves and could not see the wonder of the Promised Land that God was giving them to possess. The Israelites rejected God's instructions and paid a terrible price. They wandered in the wilderness for four decades, never receiving God's best for their lives. *They moved around, but they made no progress.*

This is like a dog that chases its own tail. It runs around and around in circles, yet it goes nowhere. Ignoring the wonders around him, the dumb dog focuses only on itself. If it finally catches up with itself . . . the results could be painful. Unless the dog passes out from sheer dizziness, the careless canine could tear it's own flesh! Worse yet, it could bite off its tail and lose an important part of its body.

Some Christians are like this (as were the Israelites of that day). However, there is one distinct difference today— *Jesus Christ.* You see, Jesus *is* Canaan! Every Christian enters Canaan when they receive Jesus as their Savior. The Christian life is birthed in a place of incredible spiritual blessings and provision. Whether we remain there and grow, or fall back, is up to us. To fall back means to take one's eyes off of Jesus, and thus, become blinded to His eternal plan. From there, the mind focuses inward and the downward spiral begins.

When the misguided believer thinks he or she has finally caught up with themselves, they usually discover they have lost touch with God . . . *and that always leads to disaster.* Some people completely miss God's divine destiny for their lives because they refuse to follow God's instructions. A whole generation of Israelites did! Physical fitness has its benefits, but I sure don't want to run in circles for the rest of my life. *Do you?*

God wanted to take the Israelites into Canaan—*together*. He wanted them to be of one mind in His will, but ten people (who were not at their spiritual best) caused a whole generation of people . . . thousands of men and women . . . to die without receiving their inheritance. *Think about it.* If there had been just ten righteous people in Sodom and Gomorrah, God would not have reduced these cities to cinders (see Genesis 18:32).

The same principle works today. Every Christian has a spiritual family—local and universal. We have the ability to live in a good land, flowing with every blessing and necessity for life. Yet, we must move together. This is God's will for us. A chain is only as strong as its weakest link. Thousands of our ancient Jewish ancestors learned this truth, *too late*. Let us learn it now, and live! Personal pitfalls play a major role in local church dysfunction. Dismembered members lead to crippled local churches.

Every Christian is responsible, personally and corporately, to adhere to the counsel of God's Word. The Bible is our ultimate authority and the basis from which the Holy Spirit works in our lives. Let us not be an unbelieving generation that wanders and dies in the wilderness, or an incomplete Body that has lopped off its own parts because we have focused on ourselves rather than our heavenly Father.

The closer we walk with God, the more He expects us to have simple, childlike hearts. We must be spiritually sensitive to avoid the confusion and deception of our time. This is why we desperately need the ministry of the Holy Spirit. He helps us to understand the Bible and live within God's pattern of order for the Christian life.

CHAPTER 4
God's Progressive Revelation

Second Timothy 3:16 records that *"all Scripture is given by inspiration of God, and is profitable"* for our learning and correction. It equips us for *"every good work."* Starting from this vantage point, we know that *every* book in the Bible has been designed to help us in our daily living. The Old and New Testaments have been designed by God to work together toward producing an end result in our lives. The Bible is God's progressive revelation.

The apostle Paul wrote in 1 Corinthians 15:46, *"However, the spiritual is not first, but the natural, and afterward the spiritual."* The Bible provides types and shadows in the Old Testament, then reveals their spiritual significance through Jesus Christ in the New Testament. Jesus is truly the *"mystery"* that has been hidden from the foundation of the world (Romans 16:25-26).

The New Testament is the Old Testament fulfilled. The Old Testament is the New Testament revealed. The types and shadows contained in the Old Testament have spiritual application today; they give us the wisdom of practical experience. God's plan of redemption unfolds from past, to present, to future.

In Paul's day, he read and preached from the Old Testament. He taught the spiritual meaning of Israel's history using the Cross of Christ as its central theme. We must apply the same principle today. Jesus Christ and His Church are the center of Old Testament types and prophecies. New Testament passages simply reveal the spiritual significance of the ancient texts (see Figure 1).

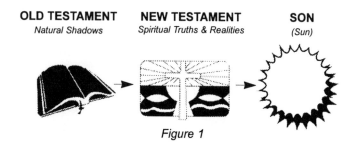

Figure 1

From The Old . . . To The New

For example, the New Testament states that born-again Christians are Jews according to the Spirit. *"For he is not a Jew who is one outwardly, nor is circumcision that which is outward in the flesh; but he is a Jew who is one inwardly; and circumcision is that of the heart, in the Spirit, not in the letter; whose praise is not from men but from God"* (Romans 2:28-29). God has given us the same covenant as His natural children. *" . . . There is no distinction between Jew and Greek, for the same Lord over all is rich to all who call upon Him"* (Romans 10:12).

This does not discount the significance of the Jewish descendants of natural Israel. God has a great plan for the Jewish people! The nation of Israel plays a *critical* role in the literal fulfillment of God's prophetic plan. When I was in Israel recently, I saw scriptures fulfilled right before my eyes. It was amazing.

When Jesus came, He preached the gospel to *"the Jew first and also for the Greek"* (Romans 1:16c). Ancient Israel rejected Jesus Christ as Messiah, so God opened the door of salvation to the Gentiles. *" 'Also the sons of the foreigner who join themselves to the Lord, to serve Him, and to love the name of the Lord, to be His servants . . . . Even them I will bring to My holy mountain, and make them joyful in My house of prayer' "* (Isaiah 56:6-7).

Brother and sister, this is you and me! We are part of God's *true* family, sealed by the Holy Spirit. Our spiritual heritage is as real as our natural heritage. In fact, it is even more real than what we understand in earthly terms. A good friend of mine, Dr. Bob Mason, shared a story with my congregation recently that powerfully illustrated the significance of our spiritual ancestry.

"I have a little boy with blond hair and blue eyes. His name is Christian Robert Mason. He's named after his first father, God, and his second father, me. Now, as most of you know, my wife Debbie was in and out of the hospital for about three years fighting against cancer. Her jaw was taken; one third of her tongue was taken; and three skin grafts were taken from her leg. She had a muscle and artery transplant from her arm into her neck; her fibula was transplanted into her jaw; she had 45 hypobaric treatments, 30 radiation treatments—and on, and on, and on . . .

"When she was in the hospital for the third or fourth time, the doctors said they couldn't save her life. Every day, Satan was saying, ' . . . I'm going to kill you. I'm going to kill you. I'm going to kill you.' ' . . . You're going to die. You're going to die. You're going to die.' Debbie would read the Word, and she'd pray. The devil told her, 'You're just doing mental calisthenics. None of that stuff works. You're going to die anyway. Why don't you just give up and forget it?'

"Right in the middle of this, God spoke to her and said, **'Not only are you going to live and not die, and declare the works of God and sing again, but you're going to have a baby boy. And he's going to have blond hair and blue eyes.'** Well, I've got brown hair and Debbie's got brown hair. I've got green eyes, and Debbie's got brown eyes. Christian has blond hair and blue eyes—just like God said he would . . . . **DN-GOD put DNA in Debbie's womb!**

"*DNA (deoxyribonucleic acid)* forms the basic material and chromosomes of the cell's nucleus. It contains the genetic code and transmits the hereditary pattern. It's the Genesis, or genetic origin, of something. Hereditary characteristics are passed down by inheritance from an ancestor to a legal heir, having right or legal title by inheritance . . .

"DNA will tell you the color of your eyes, the color of your hair, and how tall you're going to be. To some extent, DNA will tell you what your weight's going to be; your bone density, your blood type, your skin color, etc. Everything about you—a billion different things—DNA will tell you. And you're going to be that way! Now, you can take your brown hair and make it blond, but you've still got brown hair . . . . You can do a lot of things with yourself, but you're still the way God planned you to be by the DNA in your body."

I want you to know that if you are a Christian, you have received new *spiritual DNA*. By receiving Jesus Christ as your Savior, you have been *re-born* as a citizen of God's eternal Kingdom. You now have Jewish roots. You have a new heritage, new characteristics . . . and a new destiny. God broke the mold when He regenerated you and me. Try as you may, you can't change it! God has made every born-again Christian a part of His spiritual family, past, present and future.

The Adopted

"Now I say that the heir, as long as he is a child, does not differ at all from a slave, though he is master of all, but is under guardians and stewards until

the time appointed by the father. Even so we, when we were children, were in bondage under the elements of the world. But when the fullness of the time had come, God sent forth His Son, born of a woman, born under the law, to redeem those who were under the law, that we might receive the adoption as sons. And because you are sons, God has sent forth the Spirit of His Son into your hearts, crying out, 'Abba, Father!' Therefore you are no longer a slave but a son, and if a son, then an heir of God through Christ" (Galatians 4:1-7).

The Gospel age is the maturing of the Old Testament era. Old Testament believers were the *"children"* that have matured through the Gospel age into a son, of which we are a part. Romans 8:15-17 confirms, *"For you did not receive the spirit of bondage again to fear; but you received the Spirit of adoption, by whom we cry out, 'Abba Father!' The Spirit Himself bears witness with our spirit that we are children of God, and if children, then heirs—heirs of God and joint heirs with Christ . . . "*

Through the righteousness of faith, every born-again Christian has become a child of Abraham (Romans 4:13). We have been chosen by God, and grafted into His eternal family! *"Therefore it is of faith that it might be according to grace, so that the promise might be sure to all the seed, not only to those who are of the law, but also to those who are of the faith of Abraham, who is the father of us all"* (Romans 4:16).

The book of Deuteronomy 14:2 records, *" '. . . you are a holy people to the Lord your God, and the Lord has chosen you to be a people for Himself, a special treasure above all the peoples who are on the face of the earth."* First Peter 2:5 and 9 describe this passage's spiritual fulfillment, referring to believers as *"a holy priesthood"* and *"a special people"* that have been called out of darkness to proclaim God's praises in the Light of Jesus Christ.

My wife, Coral, and I now understand the concept of adoption in a living way. We recently adopted a beautiful little Russian girl and named her Alexandra Paige (we call her Alex). The experience of welcoming Alex into our hearts and home has given me a much deeper revelation of the spiritual adoption of the New Testament Church. You see, Coral and I chose Alex from all the orphans in the world to be a part of our natural family. She is now our adopted daughter and shares every right and privilege with our son by birth, Lance.

When Coral and I traveled to Russia to take custody of Alex, the court literally pulled up her Russian name and 'bleeped' it off their records—*permanently*. She was issued a new birth certificate, in the Kennedy name. Now Alex shares a family name with Coral, Lance and me. More than that, she shares our history. *Did you know that according to United States law, a parent can never disinherit an adopted child?* How does this make you feel about being adopted into God's family? I hope it makes you feel very special.

Lance is our natural child and has an important place in our hearts and plans for the future. Alex is equally as precious. The two of them complete our family unit. They are both special gifts from God that have fulfilled Coral's and my deepest hopes and dreams. Lance and Alex share the Kennedy name, a family covenant, and a future! They are equal heirs of everything that Coral and I possess. I am convinced that God views His natural and spiritual children in the same manner.

Spiritual Jerusalem

The book of Galatians 4:21-31 explains the two spiritual covenants of God's people. The *"bondwoman"* represents the old Judaistic system, or Mosaic Law. The *"freewoman"* represents *spiritual* Jerusalem, which is the Messianic Kingdom of Christ. *"But the [spiritual] Jerusalem above is free, which is the mother of us all"* (4:26). Again, this does not detract from natural Jerusalem. Israel has been and will always be the prophetic timepiece that measures the fulfillment of God's purposes in the earth. Just think of it. More than half of the prophecies recorded in the Bible have been fulfilled since Israel was declared a nation in 1948.

Jerusalem has also been likened in Scripture to the New Testament Church, *"But you have come to Mount Zion and to the city of the living God, the heavenly Jerusalem, to an innumerable company of angels, to the general assembly and church of the firstborn who are registered in heaven, to God the Judge of all, to the spirits of just men made perfect . . . "* (Hebrews 12:22-23).

If you read the passage carefully, you probably noticed that the writer used *present*, not future, tense in describing God's heavenly city and its inhabitants. Beloved, we *are* that general assembly, *right here and now!* We are the New Testament Church.

The Temple of God

Let us move a step further into God's revelation. The temple. King Solomon built the first temple in Jerusalem (see the book of 1 Kings, chapters 5 through 9). It was magnificent. This temple is the natural type of God's New Testament Church, a beautiful spiritual house comprised of many priceless elements. I believe that another temple will ultimately be built in present-day Jerusalem on the Temple Mount (according to Bible prophecy). This temple will be desecrated by the Antichrist before Jesus' triumphal return to earth when He splits the Mount of Olives (Zechariah 14:1-4).

God's spiritual temple, however, is described in the book of Ephesians (see below). It is a living organism that encompasses the universal Body of Christ. This temple will not be desecrated, but will reach complete fulfillment in Jesus' future Kingdom that will last for eternity (see Revelation 21:1-8, 22).

"You are built upon the foundation of the apostles and prophets with Christ Jesus Himself the chief Cornerstone. In Him the whole structure is joined (bound, welded) together harmoniously, and it continues to rise (grow, increase) into a holy temple in the Lord [a sanctuary dedicated, consecrated, and sacred to the presence of the Lord]. In Him [and in fellowship with one another] you yourselves also are being built up [into this structure] with the rest, to form a fixed abode (dwelling place) of God in (by, through) the Spirit" (Ephesians 2:20-22, Ampl.).

The local church is also the temple of God, as described in 1 Corinthians 3:16-17: *"Do you not discern and understand that you [the whole church at Corinth] are God's temple (His sanctuary), and that God's Spirit has His permanent dwelling in you [to be at home in you, collectively as a church and also individually]? If anyone does hurt to God's temple or corrupts it [with false doctrines] or destroys it, God will do hurt to him to the corruption of death and destroy him. For the temple of God is holy (sacred to Him) and that [temple] you [the believing church and its individual believers] are"* (Ampl.).

We are the temple of God, built with natural resources in the Old Testament and birthed in spiritual form through the Cross of Christ in the New Testament! Every Bible-believing Christian is part of a living organism that is holy to God. Knowing this, we should treat one another with the *utmost* of care and respect, because every part of God's spiritual temple—like Christ Himself—is *priceless*.

Individually, our bodies are temples of the Holy Spirit, as described in 1 Corinthians 6:19. We are part of Christ's body, therefore, we are individual parts of His spiritual temple. In the book of John, after Jesus had driven the money changers out of the temple, the Jews asked Him for a sign. Jesus replied, *" 'Destroy this temple, and in three days I will raise it up'* " (John 2:19). The words Jesus spoke were Spirit and truth, but the people did not understand Him. *Do we understand Him today?* Our bodies are temples of the Holy Spirit; earthly casings that will be transformed into vessels of glory at Christ's return (see 1 Corinthians 15:51-53 & 1 Thessalonians 4:16-18). We must be holy, even as our spiritual Father is holy (1 Peter 1:15).

The Bride of Christ

In the book of Ezekiel, the Lord spoke of His great love for Jerusalem. This text is a prophetic shadow of the New Testament Bride of Christ.

> " *'When I passed by you again and looked upon you, indeed your time was the time of love; so I spread My wing over you and covered your nakedness. Yes, I swore an oath to you and entered into a covenant with you, and you became Mine,' says the Lord God. 'Then I washed you in water: yes, I thoroughly washed off your blood, and I anointed you with oil. I clothed you in embroidered cloth and gave you sandals of badger skin; I clothed you with fine linen and covered you with silk. I adorned you with ornaments, put bracelets on your wrists, and a chain on your neck. And I put a jewel in your nose, earrings in your ears, and a beautiful crown on your head.*
>
> " *'Thus you were adorned with gold and silver, and your clothing was of fine linen, silk, and embroidered cloth. You ate pastry of fine flour, honey, and oil. You were exceedingly beautiful, and succeeded to royalty. Your fame went out among the nations because of your beauty, for it was perfect through My splendor which I had bestowed on you,' says the Lord God"* (16:8-14).

Jesus is revealed in the Gospels as the bridegroom of God's people (Matthew 9:15 & 25:1; Mark 2:19, and John 3:29). Within these passages, John the Baptist compared believers to a *"bride"* and Jesus referred to the members of His bride as *"virgins"* awaiting their groom's arrival. Yet another New Testament parallel is contained in God's instruction to Christian husbands, *". . . love your wives, just as Christ also loved the church and gave Himself for her, that He might sanctify and cleanse her with the washing of water by the word, that He might present her to Himself a glorious church, not having spot or wrinkle or any such thing, but that she should be holy and without blemish"* (Ephesians 5:25-27).

Again, the Bride of Christ will reach full maturity in the glorious days to come. New Jerusalem will descend from heaven, prepared *"as a bride adorned for her husband."* The book of Revelation also states that *we* (the nations of the redeemed) will walk in the eternal Light of this heavenly city (21:2,24).

Summing It Up

The corporate Church is the universal expression of God; local churches form local expressions of the Body of Christ. Individually, every believer is a reflection of Christ. Therefore, we should glorify God in our bodies, spirits, and churches—*because we belong to Christ.* There is no room for self-promotion or justification in the Body of Christ or within the local church.

Settle it! God's purposes have been established and will be fulfilled in and through the local and universal Church. He performs His Kingdom purposes *through* His people.

If Christians were motivated only by the natural, we would not be inspired to serve God with all our might within the framework of the local church. We would, instead, be looking only for some future move of God in the nation of

Israel. We are *spiritual* Israel. We are joint-heirs of God's covenant promises to natural Israel and are an important part of His future plans. God's family—Old and New—will reach full maturity *together*.

> *"And all of these [our Old Testament forefathers], though they won divine approval by [means of] their faith, did not receive the fulfillment of what was promised, because God had us in mind and had something better and greater in view for us, so that they [these heroes and heroines of faith] should not come to perfection apart from us [before we could join them]"* (Hebrews 11:39-40, Ampl.).

Jesus Christ removed all national barriers and natural distinctions from the redemptive dealings of God. God has one plan, and the universal Body of Christ is now part of God's plan, along with the nation of Israel. The Cross of Christ is our central theme.

Paul said in Ephesians 2:13-14, *"But now in Christ Jesus you who were once far off have been brought near by the blood of Christ. For He Himself is our peace, who has made both one, and has broken down the middle wall of separation . . . "* There is no longer a distinction between Greek or Jew, circumcised or uncircumcised . . . *Christ is all in all* (Colossians 3:11).

The Bible is clear. Christians are part of God's family on earth. We have been adopted into God's eternal Kingdom, and are part of the New Testament Jerusalem. The rich blessings of God through Jesus Christ are ours; we are part of God's *true* circumcision. Individually and collectively, we are a spiritual temple and the Bride of Christ.

I believe "the boat" is leaving. We must look at natural Israel, God's prophetic timepiece, and watch the fig leaves ripen (Matthew 24:32, Mark 13:28, and Luke 21:29-33). *Israel points the way to our glorious future in Christ!*

In the meantime, though, we had better get our "spiritual houses" in order.

The progressive revelation of God—His blueprint—extends far beyond what I am able to discuss in this mini-book. Yet, you should now understand the principle of Old Testament types and shadows and their New Testament revelations. We see the natural, but it is temporary. The natural realm is the groundwork for spiritual revelation. For the Christian, spiritual truths are reality; not the concrete "things" that are seen, felt, or experienced with the natural senses.

CHAPTER 5
The Kingdom And The Church

Just as I explored the origins of the universe, I am going to take a close look at the biblical roots of the Kingdom and the Church. These two topics are often casually discussed among Christians, but it is a sad reality that many of God's people do not understand their spiritual origins. This is the root of dysfunction. God's people must understand God's vision for His Kingdom and for the local and universal Church, as revealed in the Bible. The book of Proverbs 29:18 says, *"Where there is no vision, the people are unrestrained, but happy is he who keeps the law" (NAS).*

Today's society, at its best, is unrestrained. People are searching for spirituality without having spiritual accountability. They want to understand their spiritual nature, but they do not want absolutes governing their lives. It is the same with many of society's laws; people will always find loopholes to suit their own purposes. "Relativity is what life is all about," Society says, "Individualism is something to be strived for." *Christians beware!* This deceptive thinking began thousands of years ago when one of God's 'creations' tried to assume the role of the Creator.

> *" 'How you are fallen from heaven, O Lucifer, son of the morning! How you are cut down to the ground, you who weakened the nations! For you have said in your heart: 'I will ascend into heaven, I will exalt my throne above the stars of God; I will also sit on the mount of the congregation on the farthest sides of*

the north; I will ascend above the heights of the clouds, I will be like the Most High'" (Isaiah 14:12-14).

Lucifer desired recognition. He had his own plan and wanted to be worshipped like God; so he launched an all-out attack against God's government—*and lost*. This once beautiful creation and one third of heaven's angels were cast out of God's Kingdom for eternity. Now his name is Satan and his purpose is the same. He attacks the world just like he attacked our heavenly Father. As God's children, we must learn to *recognize* and *resist* the enemy. We must guard ourselves by learning the truth about God's Kingdom and Church. Like never before, Christians must understand their spiritual roots.

I am sure you remember the story of Noah and the ark in Genesis chapters 6 through 10. Years after God miraculously spared Noah's family from death in the worldwide flood, his descendants decided they wanted to make a name for themselves (Genesis 11:4). They forgot their spiritual roots—the reason they were alive and well. They did not keep God's vision in front of their eyes, so they stepped out of order and lost control.

The Tower of Babel—a monument to man's creative and intellectual abilities—would be built for all the world to see. It would give them a name; *status*. The people were going to make their mark by building this amazing tower that would ascend into the heavens. God was not pleased. He *"confused the language of all the earth; and from there the Lord scattered them abroad over the face of all the earth"* (Genesis 11:9). Since that time, many earthly kingdoms have risen and fallen in struggles to gain the balance of power.

Earthly Kingdoms

Earthly kingdoms assume different forms and characteristics. History tells us that one of earth's earliest forms of government emerged in ancient Greece, the same society that created the mythological gods mentioned in chapter 2. Greece began as a society of nomads, or wanderers. The people gradually developed into small city-state monarchies (one ruler), then oligarchies (a small group of rulers)—*but they never became one nation.*

In these two types of government orders, positions were generally inherited by family members. After a ruler's death, the next heir to the throne from the monarch's (or other leader's) family line would assume authority. These early forms of order were created by Greece's elite class to exercise control over the less privileged, common people.

The governments of ancient Greece were conceived by man to benefit a very few people at the expense of many. They were not established by or submitted to God's authority. Because of this, the people had divided interests and fierce competition for power and wealth existed between the Grecian city-states. As a result, the glory of ancient Greece was one of the shortest-lived cultural movements in human history.

The United States government is very different than that of ancient Greece. We are a democracy, a republic. We have one leading representative, the President, who has limited powers of authority. The real balance of power lies in the hands of the people, who elect public representatives that must answer to them. This form of order is based on the general public's desire to govern themselves and is guided by the premise that all men are created equal.

While its glory was short-lived, the influence of ancient Greece is alive and well in many world systems and government orders today. In America, we have been blessed to be a part of a democratic republic that was established on Christian principles. Yet, American Christians will tread on dangerous ground if the pursuit of life, liberty, and happiness is more important to us than pleasing our heavenly Father—Creator of the universe.

As the people of God in any country or community, we must not let the cultural trappings of an ever-shrinking world affect our perception of (and function within) God's Kingdom and Church. Ignoring God's way of doing things brings division, competition and defeat to the family of God—just like it did to ancient Greece. The Body of Christ should not function like a godless society that vanished from the face of the earth because it relied only on human thoughts and abilities.

The Sure Foundation

God's Kingdom is unlike any of man's government systems. It is far superior. His government is a theocracy, a Holy Spirit-controlled order, based on the finished work of Jesus Christ on the Cross. *"For no other foundation can anyone lay than that which is laid, which is Jesus Christ"* (1 Corinthians 3:11). The eternal government that God has instituted rests on the shoulders of our Lord, according to Isaiah 9:6-7. The Kingdom of God is the realm in which Jesus Christ reigns in the hearts of individual believers and the collective Body of Christ.

Likewise, the local church is much more than simply a place that people get inspired on Sunday mornings and midweek nights. It is not designed to be a resting area for nomads; a camp where spiritual gypsies gather to sing a few songs or hear a word that will make their day. *The local church is the spiritual home of God's people.* It is the place where God has intimate fellowship with His children and cultivates deep, meaningful relationships among His family members.

The local church is a community; a settlement of the Kingdom of God on planet earth that reflects His glory. Local churches are comprised of people who have been "called out" to do God's business because He is Lord.

Just as God brought order to a formless, shapeless void and created the universe, He has also structured the spiritual Kingdom, Church and local churches. God always gives order and beauty to His creation. If any believer dares to deny the fact that God wants to govern His people, he or she is standing on shaky ground. It is the spirit of Antichrist that attempts to break down God's order and authority. A Christian that is deceived by this spirit will deny, in word and deed, the existence of God's order and be subject to crippling dysfunction instead of overcoming victory in these Last Days.

God's Kingdom Order

The word *"kingdom"* is derived from the Greek root, *"basileia."* It means *"sovereignty, royal power, and dominion"* (Strong's 932 & 935). God's Kingdom is the realm of His leadership and authority. As Christians, we are God's willing subjects. His Kingdom rules and directs every aspect of our lives: spiritual, financial, social, economic and otherwise. Let us take a look at several important aspects of the Kingdom of God.

The Kingdom Of God is the sphere of God's rule in the earth, as manifested in the hearts of individual believers and within the local church. The book of Isaiah 9:6 & 7a prophesied, *". . . and the government will be upon His shoulder . . . Of the increase of His government and peace there will be no end . . . "* Paul confirmed in the book of Ephesians that Christ's power *is "far above all principality and power and might and dominion, and every name that is named, not only in this age but also in that which is to come. And He put all things under His feet, and gave Him to be head over all things to the church, which is His body, the fullness of Him who fills all in all"* (1:21-23).

Jesus' authority over the Church and local churches is also demonstrated in the book of Revelation (see chapters 1-3 & 22:12-17). Jesus has the authority to commend, rebuke, instruct and deliver Kingdom promises to His people, as represented through His government order within the local church. He rules where His leadership and authority are acknowledged. *He does not rule with the iron hand of a monarch, nor does He negotiate like a Western diplomat.* Every Christian has an equal opportunity to obey Him as He leads us from level-to-level in our walks of faith. *Jesus—the Word that was made flesh for all men—makes His living Word flesh in the hearts and lives of everyone that willingly submits to Him.*

In the book of Acts, Peter and the apostles of the early church demonstrated a real understanding of Christ's Kingdom rulership when they responded to an order to not preach the Gospel. They declared, " *'We ought to obey God rather than men.'* " (5:29). Peter later wrote about the result of a submitted life—

"But sanctify the Lord God in your hearts, and always be ready to give a defense to everyone who asks you a reason for the hope that is in you, with meekness and fear; having a good conscience, that when they defame you as evildoers, those who revile your good conduct in Christ may be ashamed" (1 Peter 3:15-16).

The Kingdom of God is His rule in the heavenly realm. The book of 1 Peter 3:22 records that Christ *"has gone into heaven and is at the right hand of God, angels and authorities and powers having been made subject to Him."* This is the reason Jesus instructed the people to pray *" . . . Our Father in heaven, hallowed be Your name. Your kingdom come. Your will be done on earth as it is in heaven"* (Matthew 6:9-10).

Christ gives His authority to believers that submit to His Kingdom rulership. This authority begins in the natural world, and also affects the heavenly realm. *"And I will give you the keys of the kingdom of heaven, and whatever you bind on earth will be bound in heaven, and whatever you loose on earth will be loosed in heaven"* (Matthew 16:19). Christians have the authority to take dominion over demons (Luke 10:17 & Mark 15:15), angels (1 Corinthians 6:3), the world (Genesis 1:26-28, 1 Corinthians 6:2, and Revelation 20:4), and sin (Romans 6:11-14 & 8:2, 1 Corinthians 15:34, and 1 John 3:9). *God's people can do all things through the strength and authority of Christ!*

The Kingdom of God is not limited by time or dimension. The Kingdom of God is *permanent*. It is not only a past and present reality, but will reach its ultimate maturity and prophetic fulfillment in the future. As Paul was approaching the end of his earthly ministry, he wrote that he had fought *"a good fight"* (2 Timothy 4:7), knowing the Lord would deliver and preserve him *"for His heavenly kingdom"* (verse 18).

Paul looked toward his divine redemption and rewards, having already submitted to Kingdom rule and exercised Kingdom authority through Jesus Christ on the earth. In the book of Matthew, chapter 8, Jesus marveled at the faith of the Centurion when he asked Him to merely *"speak a word"* to heal his servant (verse 8). Of this man and those like him, Jesus declared that *". . . many will come from east and west, and sit down with Abraham, Isaac, and Jacob in the kingdom of heaven"* (verse 11).

Just as surely as we will experience it in the future, the Kingdom of God is as strong a reality right now in the spiritual dimension. Paul said in the book of Romans 14:17, *". . . the kingdom of God is not eating and drinking, but righteousness and peace and joy in the Holy Spirit."* He was instructing the Christians in Rome to be guided by God's heavenly wisdom instead of using fleshly reasoning in their relationships with others. In every area of Christian life, the Kingdom of God must have authority over the thoughts and actions of the believer.

The Kingdom of God reigns within us; it is not an external kingdom, like the kingdoms of the natural world.

Throughout history, earthly kingdoms have either been built or have fallen because of divided interests and struggles for power. Jesus said, *" 'My kingdom is not of this world . . . ' "* (John 18:36). It does not function like world governments. It cannot be perceived in the same way, or on the same level, that earthly kingdoms are understood. *The Kingdom authority of Jesus Christ will never change hands.* It is a *permanent reality* that will continue even after the earth passes away (see Revelation 21).

The Kingdom of God is progressively revealed. John the Baptist prepared the way for Jesus by announcing the Kingdom was *"at hand"* (Matthew 3:2). At that time, he was speaking to people that had not yet seen or heard the true Messiah. John called for repentance and pointed the way to the Kingdom that would soon be revealed through Jesus Christ (see John 1). He prepared the way for the Gospel, just as the Holy Spirit prepares an unbeliever's heart to receive Jesus.

When a person receives Jesus as their Savior, they are adopted into God's Kingdom and the universal Body of Christ. Kingdom provisions and promises can then be called upon and received by the believer as they are needed. Jesus said to Nicodemus—*" '. . . unless one is born again, he cannot see the kingdom of God' "* (John 3:3). This means that if you are born again, you *can* see God's Kingdom! When Jesus is the Lord of your heart, you automatically inherit the ability to perceive, understand and function within His Kingdom realm.

The Kingdom is also revealed through the acts and manifestations of God. Chapter 12 of the book of Matthew describes what it means when God sovereignly performs a supernatural act, such as when Jesus healed a demon-possessed man in verse 22. Jesus answered the wicked thoughts of the Pharisees by saying, *" 'But if I cast out demons by the Spirit of God, surely the kingdom of God has come upon you' "* (verse 28).

Jesus suffered persecution during His time on earth and warned that His people would also be persecuted, especially in the Last Days. This Kingdom truth invariably comes to light when a believer takes a stand for the cause of Christ. *We are in the world, beloved, not of the world* (John 17:14). After being stoned by Jewish people in Greece (and *miraculously* recovering), Paul said boldly to the believers there, *" 'We must through many tribulations enter the kingdom of God.' "* (Acts 14:22).

As Kingdom rule grows within a believer's heart, the grace of God directs and empowers that person to do His will—even what would seem to be impossible. *All things are possible to them that believe* (Mark 9:23). God's grace strengthens and transforms the submitted Christian into the image of Christ, from *"faith to faith"* (Romans 1:17) and from *"glory to glory"* (2 Corinthians 3:18). This means as you submit to God's Kingdom rule, you *will* reach new spiritual levels in Christ—*guaranteed*. Take rest in the wise words of the apostle Paul, who declared in the book of Philippians, *". . . He who has begun a good work in you will complete it until the day of Jesus Christ"* (1:6).

The Kingdom of God will have no end. At the close of the present age, Jesus will submit Himself and His Kingdom to the Father. Every part of creation, including the vast stretches of the universe, will come under complete subjection to God. The Kingdom identified by type and shadow in the Old Testament and revealed in the New Testament will reach *full maturity*. According to Scripture, it will become in its truest sense, the everlasting Kingdom of God.

> *"Then comes the end, when He delivers the kingdom to God the Father, when He puts an end to all rule and all authority and power. For He must reign until He has put all enemies under His feet. The last enemy that will be destroyed is death. For 'He has put all things under His feet.' But when He says 'all things are put under Him,' it is evident that He who put all things under Him is excepted. Now when all*

things are made subject to Him, then the Son Himself will also be subject to Him who put all things under Him, that God may be all in all." (1 Corinthians 15:24-28).

The book of Revelation describes our glorious future. At the beginning of the everlasting age of God's Kingdom, New Jerusalem will descend from heaven and rest upon the soils of a new earth. The city will shine with the glory of God, with the clear brilliance of a precious stone. There will be no temple in New Jerusalem because God Almighty and the Lamb will be our temple. Night will not fall on this city for eternity because the glory of God will illuminate it. The crystal-clear River of Life will flow from the throne of God and of the Lamb, and the fruit of the Tree of Life will bring healing to the nations (see Revelation 21 & 22).

Summing It Up

When considering the magnificent future Kingdom that God has prepared for everyone who loves and obeys Him, the earthly kingdoms we know after the flesh pale in comparison (as do the challenges we face every day). Earthly practices and cares are of little significance to the believer that keeps his or her eyes focused on Jesus—the author and finisher of our faith and our hope of glory! The Light that will illuminate New Jerusalem can enlighten your heart today, and lead you on to victory.

Second Corinthians 4:16-18 says, *"Therefore we do not lose heart. Even though our outward man is perishing, yet the inward man is being renewed day by day. For our light affliction, which is but for a moment, is working for us a far more exceeding and eternal weight of glory, while we do not look at the things which are seen, but the things which are not seen. For the things which are seen are temporary, but the things which are not seen are eternal."*

Kingdom Order And The Church

The Kingdom and the Church are intimately related; they are blended together as part and parcel of the same package. Remember, God *synthesizes*. He works all things *together*. Separating the Kingdom from the universal and local church can cripple a person's ability to *hear* and *apply* the Word of God. It would be like trying to weave a multi-colored, multi-textured fabric with just one color and weight of thread . . . *it just will not work!* As God's children, we must follow His example and weave together the amazing truths that make up the Kingdom and the Church.

Strong local bodies of believers are a Kingdom emphasis, yet we are living in a period of history where the importance of the local church and biblical church government are being de-emphasized. Local churches are *not* going out of style! As revealed in chapter 4, strong local churches are God's *permanent* order for this age. They are a vital aspect of God's pattern and plan for evangelizing the world and bringing His people to spiritual maturity.

The Mystical And The Concrete

The Church has two different forms; the *mystical* and the *concrete*. Jesus used the term "church" only two times; both in the book of Matthew. In these Scriptures, He distinguished between the two types of churches. Christ's description of the *mystical* Church appears in Matthew 16:18, and refers to the universal Body of Christ (see also Ephesians 1:22-23 & Hebrews 12:23):

> " *'And I also say to you that you are Peter, and on this rock I will build My church, and the gates of Hades shall not prevail against it.'* "

Jesus referred to the *concrete* (or local) church in Matthew 18:15-17, when He talked about dealing with problems among believers. " *'Moreover if your brother sins against you, go and tell him his fault between you and him alone. If he hears you, you have gained your brother. But if he will not hear, take with you one or two more, that "by the mouth of two or three witnesses every word may be established." And if he refuses to hear them, tell it to the church. But if he refuses even to hear the church, let him be to you like a heathen and a tax collector.'"* There are other New Testament passages that refer to the local church, such as when Paul and Barnabas *"appointed elders in every church"* in Acts 14:23. Paul also wrote in the book of 1 Corinthians that he taught *"everywhere in every church"* (4:17).

The understanding of the *concrete* church consisting of real people with real human needs is where *effective* ministry *must* begin. Practical, tangible, ministry cannot take place where there is only a *mystical* vision. I would say that many Christians today are frustrated in their ministries because they have not discerned their relationship to a visible— *local*—Body of Christ. The person who says they are a member of the Body of Christ, yet is not part of a local church family, is living in contradiction. (This is like saying they are a member of the human race, but do not have a natural family.) It is ungrounded, unhealthy, and contrary to the Word of God.

The Church Throughout The Ages

The word *"church"* is derived from the Greek root, *"ekklesia,"* which *means "a calling out, a popular meeting, especially a religious congregation"* (Strong's 1577). Its Old Testament counterpart in the Hebrew language is the word *"assembly"* (Strong's 6951 & 5712). Both of these words refer to the people of God assembling or gathering together before the Lord. Yet, there are distinct differences between New and Old Testament practices of worship. To gain a better understanding of the New Testament Church and its relationship to Old Testament types, one must understand it's stages of development. There have been five progressive stages of development for the Church and local churches.

Stage One: The Church was foreshadowed in the Old Testament. As I discussed in great detail in Chapter 4, the Old Testament is filled with types and shadows of the New Testament Church. First the natural, then the spiritual. The Church is the adopted family of God, spiritual Jerusalem, God's temple, and His glorious Bride. Isaiah's prophecy in chapter 43, verses 1, 5 and 7, confirms this. *"But now, thus says the Lord, who created you, O Jacob, and He who formed you, O Israel: 'Fear not, for I have redeemed you; I have called you by your name; you are Mine . . . . Fear not, for I am with you; I will bring your descendants from the east, and gather you from the west; I will say to the north, "Give them up!" and to the south, "Do not keep them back!" Bring My sons from afar, and My daughters from the ends of the earth—Everyone who is called by My name, whom I have created for My glory; I have formed him, yes, I have made him.'"*

The apostle Paul wrote in the book of Ephesians, *" . . . by revelation He made known to me the mystery . . . which in other ages was not made known to the sons of men, as it has now been revealed by the Spirit to His holy apostles and prophets: that the Gentiles should be fellow heirs, of the same body, and partakers of His promise in Christ through the gospel . . . . and [for Paul] to make all see what is the fellowship of the mystery, which from the beginning of the ages has been hidden in God who created all things through Jesus Christ; to the intent that now the manifold wisdom of God might be made known <u>by the church</u> to the principalities and powers in the heavenly places, according to the eternal purpose which He accomplished in Christ Jesus our Lord" (3:3-11).*

As fellow heirs of the Kingdom of God, the Body of Christ has been "called out" to do His business and accomplish His purpose in the heavens and on the earth. God knew you and me before He created the heavens and the earth, and has pre-determined that we would complete what He started through our spiritual ancestors.

Stage Two: The Church has been instituted by Christ. The New Testament Church was birthed through the life and ministry of the Lord, Jesus Christ, *". . . Who has saved us and called us with a holy calling, not according to our works, but according to his own purpose and grace which was given to us in Christ Jesus before time began . . . "* (2 Timothy 1:9).

The book of Genesis 3:15 contains the first Messianic prophecy in the Old Testament. In this passage, Jesus was identified by type as the Seed of the woman put in conflict with the seed of the serpent. It states, *"And I will put enmity between you and the woman, and between your seed and her Seed [Jesus]; He shall bruise your head, and you shall bruise His heel."* The conflict between the Church and Satan is restated in Ephesians 1:23, which teaches that Jesus is the head of the Church and that all things have been put *"under His feet"* (see previous section, God's Kingdom Order).

Jesus Christ *is* the greatest revelation in God's plan of the ages! He is the Mystery of old and the Revealer of the glorious things to come. Hebrews 1:1-2 states, *"God, who at various times and in various ways spoke in time past to the fathers by the prophets, has in these last days spoken to us by His Son, whom He has appointed heir of all things . . . "*

Jesus is the fulfillment of Old Testament types and prophecies and the author of spiritual order within the Church and local churches. This is revealed in His words to Peter in Matthew 16:18, *" . . . on this rock I will build my church."* Jesus was not talking about a brand new plan! He was speaking of a transition from type to anti-type; shadow to substance; natural to spiritual.

Let me explain. In the book of Exodus 33:18-23 (and chapter 34), Moses had an encounter with God. Israel had been delivered out of Egypt and was settled in the wilderness of Sinai. God was in the process of establishing a new order for His people. When Moses obeyed God and stood in the rocky cleft of that mountain, God passed His glory over him. It was on this rock that Moses received the Ten Commandments, which he later delivered to the children of Israel.

The New Testament counterpart of this "rock" experience is simply the revelation of Jesus Christ and its public confession. When Peter boldly confessed in Matthew 16:16, " *'You are the Christ, the Son of the living God,'* " Jesus re-established His Church . . . *and* is still building it today.

Stage Three: The Church is structured by the Holy Spirit. The Old Testament "wineskins" have passed away and the time of the "new wine" has come! The New Testament Church was not birthed by God to be directed by man's power. It must be fueled by the power of the Holy Spirit! The book of 1 Corinthians 12:12-13 says, *"For as the body is one and has many members, but all the members of that one body, being many, are one body, so also is Christ. For by one Spirit we were all baptized into one body—whether Jews or Greeks, whether slaves or free—and have all been made to drink into one Spirit."*

The Holy Spirit is the administrator of the local church; He has established an organizational structure (or offices) that brings health and vitality to God's family. For the purposes of this mini-book, I will briefly review the basics. First, elders must be ordained in every church, according to Acts 14:23, *"So when they had appointed elders in every church, and prayed with fasting, they commended them to the Lord in whom they had believed."* In my congregation, the local elders are referred to as Touch Pastors. They serve pastoral roles in the North Church's home cell group ministry and also teach. The book of Ephesians 4:11 provides a list of the offices within the category of elders. It includes:

- Apostles
- Prophets
- Evangelists

- Pastors
- Teachers

Deacons are the next level of local church leadership. They are "servants" within the local church. (At the North Church, deacons are referred to as CARE Leaders, an acronym in the home cell ministry which stands for "Caring And Reaching Everyone.") Deacons carry the physical aspects of the ministry, much like the priests that served Aaron and his sons in the book of Numbers 18:2-4. The sixth chapter of Acts, verses 1-4, tells more about the ministry of deacons.

The organizational structure of the local church can be likened to the skeletal system of the human body. The skeleton gives definite shape and form to the body. It makes the body solid, stable and permanent. It supports the organs, helping them to function properly as a unit, and facilitates proper movement of the body's parts. The skeleton cannot move without the body and the body cannot move without the skeleton.

This is how the Holy Spirit works. He distributes ministry gifts to God's people and empowers them to do His will. The Christian's responsibility is to submit to the Holy Spirit's leadership in order to please God and be productive for His Kingdom. Romans 12:4-8 says, *"For as we have many members in one body, but all the members do not have the same function, so we, being many, are one body in Christ, and individually members of one another . . . "*

> *"Having then gifts differing according to the grace that is given to us, let us use them: if prophecy, let us prophesy in proportion to our faith; or ministry, let us use it in our ministering; he who teaches, in teaching; he who exhorts, in exhortation; he who gives, with liberality; he who leads, with diligence; he who shows mercy, with cheerfulness."*

Each part of the Body of Christ has been designed to compliment and complete the other parts. *It is critical, therefore, that you learn your function in God's family.* This will exercise your faith in God and release others to operate in their God-given functions. The family of God is a spiritual organism; we must let the attributes of the Holy Spirit flow through us. When we submit to the Holy Spirit, God's anointing and blessings are released. First Corinthians 12:7 says, *"But the manifestation of the Spirit is given to each one for the profit of all . . . "*

The bottom line is the Holy Spirit determines who does what in the church, and for what period of time. If you do not know your ministry gift or office within the local church, ask the Holy Spirit to reveal it to you. He will direct you. He will give you an inner witness, then confirm it through the church leadership, or (if you are called to be a minister) by the laying on of hands of the presbytery.

As children of God, our desire must be to build the Kingdom of God within the framework of the biblical leadership structure established for the local church. This is not legalism, but a means to effectively tap the full potential of every believer. True biblical oversight brings incredible release and liberty to God's people. It facilitates and supports Body ministry *and* the individual priesthood of the submitted Christian (these two areas, by the way, work hand-in-hand).

Psalm 133:1-3 illustrates how God releases anointing and blessing to His people.

> *"Behold, how good and how pleasant it is for brethren to dwell together in unity! It is like the precious oil upon the head, running down on the beard, the beard of Aaron, running down on the edge of his garments. It is like the dew of Hermon, descending upon the mountains of Zion; for there the Lord commanded the blessing—life forevermore."*

God's anointing oil began at the top of Aaron's head, then ran down his beard until it reached the edges of his priestly garments. This image represents the proper flow of order within the local church. The Holy Spirit directs God's people, from leadership to laity, with the anointing of the Holy Spirit flowing in perfect symmetry. As a Kingdom of priests, Christians are responsible to follow God's pattern for life and ministry.

Stage Four: The Church has suffered due to false doctrine and spiritual decline. Human history and the Word of God confirm this fact. Just as there were periods of captivity for natural Israel, there have also been dark periods in the history of the Church. When God's people sinned through disobedience, rebellion, or unbelief, they suffered the consequences of their actions. There have been times when God's people were literally turned over to their enemies! The spirit is willing, but the flesh is weak. This is why we must be watchful and pray without ceasing (Matthew 26:41, 2 Timothy 4:5, and 1 Peter 4:7).

The book of 1 John 4:1-3 states, *"Beloved, do not believe every spirit, but test the spirits, whether they are of God; because many false prophets have gone out into the world. By this you know the Spirit of God: every spirit that confesses that Jesus Christ has come in the flesh is of God, and every spirit that does not confess that Jesus Christ has come in the flesh is not of God. And this is the spirit of the Antichrist, which you have heard was coming, and is now already in the world."*

Any Christian that fails to recognize the Antichrist spirit has a strong influence in today's society is deceiving themselves. The name of our precious Lord, Jesus Christ, is denounced on a daily basis! This does not surprise God. It is part of what must take place before Jesus returns to win the final victory in the battle of good and evil (Revelation 20:7-10).

The book of 2 Peter 2:1-3 records, *"But there were also false prophets among the people, even as there will be false teachers among you, who will secretly bring in destructive heresies, even denying the Lord who bought them, and bring on themselves swift destruction. And many will follow their destructive ways, because of whom the way of truth will be blasphemed. By covetousness they will exploit you with deceptive words; for a long time their judgment has not been idle, and their destruction does not slumber."* These *"ravenous wolves"* will be known by their fruits (Matthew 7:15-20). Jesus said in Matthew 13, verses 18-30 and 36-43, that He would not separate the *"wheat"* from the *"tares"* until the end of the age.

Some churches today have been infiltrated by the Antichrist spirit. If this were not true, the Last Day church in Revelation 2:4-5 would not have received this warning,

" '. . . I have this against you, that you have left your first love. Remember therefore from where you have fallen; repent and do the first works, or else I will come to you quickly and remove your lampstand from its place—unless you repent.' "

Many Bible scholars have believed the seven churches listed in chapters 2 and 3 of the book of Revelation are prophetic of conditions that would come to pass in the distant future of their writing. These conditions included spiritual poverty and blasphemy (2:9), false doctrine and fornication (2:14), teachings and idolatry of Jezebel (2:20), and lukewarmness and spiritual blindness (3:15-16). *Could we be living in that time today?* Take a look around, and decide for yourself.

The books of 2 Thessalonians and 2 Timothy also describe events that will take place during the Last Days. The first prophecy describes the great "falling away." Many people will be deceived before the son of perdition is revealed (2 Thessalonians 2:1-3). Second Timothy 3:12-13 warns about the Last Days, *"Yes, and all who desire to live godly in Christ Jesus will suffer persecution. But evil men and impostors will grow worse and worse, deceiving and being deceived."*

Do you know what it means to be persecuted? If not, do you know what to expect? Let me tell you. In the Greek language, it means *"to pursue . . . ensue . . . press toward"* (Strong's 1377). This same word in English means *"to oppress with ill treatment . . . . To annoy persistently; bother"* (The American Heritage College Dictionary). The enemy is pursuing God's people in these Last Days, constantly pestering us with one little thing or the other—*to get our eyes off of Jesus.* He wants to turn our attention, and hearts, away from our Lord. We must *recognize* and *resist* the spirit of Antichrist.

It is time for every child of God to stand firm and take heart—being fully aware of the deception of our times. Reading further in 2 Timothy 3:14, we are instructed, *". . . you must continue in the things which you have learned and been assured of, knowing from whom you have learned them."* To stand in the midst of turbulent times, you must be planted in a strong Bible-centered local church where you know the people who labor among you (1 Thessalonians 5:12).

As the world grows darker and darker, God's glory will become brighter and brighter in the Last Day Church! For those with hearing ears and upright hearts toward God, there is hope for a glorious tomorrow.

Stage Five: The Church is being restored in the Last Days. Both the Old and New Testaments foretell the restoration of the Church. The book of Acts 15:13-17 says, *"And after they had become silent, James answered, saying, 'Men and brethren, listen to me: Simon has declared how God at the first visited the Gentiles to take out of them a people for His name. And with this the words of the prophets agree, just as it is written: "After this I will return and will rebuild the tabernacle of David, which has fallen down; I will rebuild its* *ruins, and I will set it up; so that the rest of mankind may seek the Lord, even all the Gentiles who are called by My name, says the Lord who does all these things" '*

In this passage of Acts, James was quoting a prophecy contained in the book of Amos 9:11-12. There are other Old Testament passages that speak of a Latter Day restoration of the Church. The books of Ezra and Nehemiah draw a prophetic parallel between the Church's restoration and the ancient Jewish people being restored to Israel. Other Scriptures can be found in Psalm 69:35, 102:13-16, 126:1-6, 132:13-18, and Isaiah 4:2-6.

As mentioned earlier, the restored church has been described in Scripture as God's glorious Bride *"without spot or wrinkle."* The Holy Spirit is preparing God's people to receive their Groom. The book of Revelation 19:6-8 declares:

> *"And I heard, as it were, the voice of a great multitude, as the sound of many waters and as the sound of many thunderings, saying, 'Alleluia! For the Lord God Omnipotent reigns! Let us be glad and rejoice and give Him glory, for the marriage of the Lamb has come, and His wife has made herself ready.' And to her it was granted to be arrayed in fine linen, clean and bright, for the fine linen is the righteous acts of the saints."*

God is perfecting us. According to Philippians 2:13, He is working in you and me to will and to do His good pleasure—*to perform righteous acts in His name.* We are part of the *"great mystery"* of Christ! You see, Jesus took human form to overcome sin. He then made the Church a living organism to rescue sinners. This spiritual family receives wisdom, direction and power from the Holy Spirit. . . . *And* the Spirit is constantly preparing and perfecting God's people on earth for our wedding feast with Jesus in heaven.

Yes, a great falling away is taking place, and evil is intensifying in the earth—but that is just *one side* of the story! Many of the things that are happening today are actually the hand of God shaking the earth (see Hebrews 12:25-29). False systems and religious movements that have rejected the move of the Holy Spirit are being shaken to their foundations. *God has ordered this process because Jesus Christ is the one, true, foundation of order* (1 Corinthians 3:11). It is only the power and authority of Jesus that crushes the enemy's head under our feet (see Romans 16:20, Hebrews 2:14, and Revelation 12).

God is in the process of drawing every person to Himself that will love and serve Him with an undivided heart. There is no longer room for divided interests and careless individualism in the Body of Christ. We were not created to function like the kingdoms of this world! We must join together in love and unity, and become everything God has created us to be. *Jesus is adorning His Bride—a people that will be a praise in the earth—to manifest His Kingdom, power and glory to the nations.*

CHAPTER 6
Biblical Principles
of Spiritual Growth And Order

There cannot be a glorious church without glorious saints! Strong local churches are the result of strong local believers functioning in proper order at every level of ministry. Let me share with you a few principles that I believe facilitate individual health, growth and order, and contribute to healthy local churches and a harmonious, effective, Body of Christ.

Living Unto The Lord

The first chapter of the book of Acts contains a principle that is essential to individual spiritual growth and proper function within local church bodies. It is an interesting passage because it says something different than what many believers may think. In verse 8, Jesus said, *"But you shall receive power when the Holy Spirit has come upon you; and you shall be witnesses to Me in Jerusalem, and in all Judea and Samaria, and to the end of the earth."*

This passage states that we will be witnesses to Him! It does not say we will be witnesses to them. So often, I have seen well-meaning believers that love the Lord trying to be witnesses *to them*—the world. *Jesus wants us to live our lives in faith toward Him.* Exercising faith toward God means living unto the Lord; desiring to please God with our every thought, word and action. It is possible for you to live a life of integrity, righteousness and holiness—*not by living unto the world*—but by living a life of faith that is pleasing to God.

Earlier in the first chapter of Acts, Jesus had commanded the disciples to wait in Jerusalem for the promise of the Father. In their earthly wisdom, the disciples responded by asking Jesus when power and authority would be restored to Israel (verse 6). They wanted to know when they could exercise power over the people that had cruelly oppressed them. The disciples wanted to put their enemies in their rightful place and be rightly recognized as God's chosen people. At this point, the disciples' faith was not toward God. Their focus was on earthly things instead of Jesus, and this preoccupation clouded their perception of God's eternal plan.

Let us examine our hearts. Do we hunger and thirst for the righteousness of God, or do we seek only to defend our own interests and put others (right or wrong as they may be) in their rightful place? Jesus told the disciples that the times and seasons God put in His own authority were not for them to know (verse 7). Therefore, we should not let the desire for position, authority, or recognition direct our thoughts and actions.

True power (abundance, ability, strength and might) is given by the Holy Spirit to every believer that desires to be a *witness*—a living testimony that bears record of the life of Christ. It is this Light that shines from within us and influences the people around us, in our communities, cities, nations, and ultimately . . . the world.

Completing One Another in Love

Another key principle that brings order within the local church and individual believers can be found in the book of Ephesians 4:16. This passage describes the Body of Christ as one organism—*" . . . joined and knit together by what every joint supplies, according to the effective working by which every part does its share, causes growth of the body for the edifying of itself in love."* Christians have been designed by God to *complete* one another—not to compete with each other! If you consider yourself a believer, you must work hand-in-hand with your brothers and sisters in Christ. You must seek the good of others at all times. This is God's will for you.

In a humble attitude of faith toward God, we must accept and respect each person and their function within the Body of Christ. We are members of one another, whether we like it or not! We are incomplete without each other. If we try to function independently, or hinder another person's function, we will step out of order and be subject to God's correction. The Lord blesses unity; *nothing less*. Paul's closing words to the Corinthians confirm this.

> *"Finally, brethren, farewell. Become complete. Be of good comfort, be of one mind, live in peace; and the God of love and peace will be with you"* (2 Corinthians 13:11).

The apostle Paul also exhorted believers in the twelfth chapter of Romans to *"be kindly affectionate to one another with brotherly love, in honor giving preference to one another"* (verse 10). When we go above-and-beyond the call of duty to accept and love our spiritual family, giving honor to them, *God honors us*.

I can remember a misguided attempt I made in Bible college to set things straight with a fellow student. This brother had been picking on my roommate, and I was angry with him. He was dishonoring my friend, so I was going to put him in his place. In short, I beat him up. I reacted to my brother's weakness instead of preferring him in a spirit of love and acceptance. I was young in my walk of faith and did not understand that I was making a terrible mistake.

The fact that the young man was wrong in his approach to my roommate did not justify my actions. Nor will someone else's sin justify your actions if you let anger (or any other fruit of darkness) control you. The Bible tells us in

Ephesians 4:26 that anger is not a license to sin. If you have truly died to self, just as Christ died on the Cross, anger will not cause you to sin because your own works are dead. When the 'self' has not been crucified, people devalue others and give place to the devil. Romans 12:3 says,

"For I say, through the grace given to me, to everyone who is among you, not to think of himself more highly than he ought to think, but to think soberly, as God has dealt to each one a measure of faith."

It takes faith to properly discern God's family! *What does this mean?* It means keeping right relationships with each other. Those that do not guard their relationships become guilty of the sin outlined in 1 Corinthians 11:29-30, *"For he who eats and drinks [the Lord's Supper] in an unworthy manner eats and drinks judgment to himself, not discerning the Lord's body. For this reason many are weak and sick among you, and many sleep."* You see, God cannot accept the spiritual offering of a person that willingly harbors bad relationships. In Matthew 5:21-24, Jesus exposed the roots of this predicament—murder. He then told the multitudes, *" 'Therefore if you bring your gift to the altar, and there remember that your brother has something against you, leave your gift there before the altar, and go your way. First be reconciled to your brother, and then come and offer your gift.' "*

Some people that God deeply loves suffer or even die because they have failed to properly discern the Body of Christ.

Let us test our own actions, *"For if we would judge ourselves, we would not be judged.... Let each one examine his own work, and then he will have rejoicing in himself alone, and not in another"* (1 Corinthians 11:31 & Galatians 6:4). You can rejoice before God when *you* have chosen to do His will, but you cannot make this choice for anyone else!

God holds each person accountable for their own words and actions, and He honors people that pursue the will of God in their relationships.

"He who is slow to anger is better than the mighty, and he who rules his spirit than he who takes a city" (Proverbs 16:32).

When you are tempted to put someone in their place, remember your own shortcomings and submit to the guidance of the Holy Spirit. He will show you how to handle your problems, step-by-step. He will give you the words and actions that will bring life, not death, to your relationships. Remember, we have been created by God to *complete* each other, not to compete with one another. God alone knows and determines the true place of every believer.

Fulfilling The Law of Christ

At the North Church we live by the motto, *"We are a large family of many friends, caring for each other."* We understand what it means to be one family in Christ—to love others as we love ourselves. True love is kind. It protects, trusts, hopes and perseveres when everyone else has given up (see 1 Corinthians 13). Love overlooks weaknesses and gives people that may have been totally wrong the opportunity to make things right.

By carrying one another's burdens, we fulfill the law of Christ (Galatians 6:2). We must compensate for one another's faults just like the physical body compensates for injuries and weaknesses within its members. *Believe it or not, there are no perfect human beings on the face of the earth.* Not even you! The perfect One is sitting at the right hand of our heavenly Father, making intercession for us.

In kind, we should confess our faults to one another and pray for each other so that we can be healed (James 5:16). We compensate for weaknesses in our Body by loving, accepting and preferring one another and taking our burdens to the Cross. A chain is only as strong as its weakest link. Therefore, we must choose at every opportunity to strengthen and uplift our brethren.

Walking Softly with God

The third principle that promotes individual spiritual growth and facilitates order within the universal and local church is illustrated in the book of 1 Kings 6:7. *"And the temple, when it was being built, was built with stone finished at the quarry, so that no hammer or chisel or any iron tool was heard in the temple while it was being built."*

In other words, the bricks that were used to build King Solomon's temple were pre-designed and trued in a refining process that allowed them to be set into place *without force*. At the end of the refining process, each brick had been perfected so that it complimented and completed the bricks around it. Believers undergo a similar refining process. It's called the testing of our faith, which produces patience. *"But let patience have its perfect work, that you may be perfect and complete, lacking nothing"* (James 1;4).

Every believer must fit, without friction, stress or frustration, into God's assigned place for them within the local church and the Body of Christ. This truing process proves our faith in the Lord. I call it walking softly with God. First Thessalonians 5:14 exhorts believers to *". . . warn those who are unruly, comfort the fainthearted, uphold the weak, be patient with all."* When we wake up each morning, we should look in the mirror and remember that God is in the process of perfecting us. A *custom-designed* product requires a tremendous amount of detail work to bring it to perfection!

A Word To Pastors

For pastors, the truing process begins as we allow the Holy Spirit to add people to our church. I often say to my congregation, *"If I add you, I've got to keep you. If God adds you, there is nothing I can do to run you off."* You see, if pastors add people to their churches, it's manipulation. If God adds them, it's a spiritual multiplication. When God adds people to a church, they are planted in the location that will foster their growth and development in God's Kingdom. They are in the will of God in the local church.

The second phase of the pastoral truing process involves leadership, mentorship and discipleship. *Godly leaders must exercise patience.* They must never be in a hurry to assign titles or responsibilities to a person—no matter how gifted and talented that person may be. The Holy Spirit will *raise up* the people He has *anointed* to fulfill each function. This takes the pressure off of you! A person's function becomes obvious when he or she begins *doing* the work. It is then that you can help shape and develop a believer's gifts and abilities, and most importantly, their Godly character.

Great patience is required in pastoral care and oversight! The first sign of a true apostle, as stated in 2 Corinthians 12:12, is great patience. *"Truly the signs of an apostle were accomplished among you with all perseverance, in signs and wonders and mighty deeds."* The ability to perform signs, wonders and miracles came *after* the apostle exercised much patience. A pastor must let the Holy Spirit build the local church through him, molding and shaping the people to fit, without force, into God's spiritual house.

A Word To God's People

The truing process for laity begins by attending the church where the Holy Spirit plants you. Remember, God knows where you will function and develop to your fullest potential in the Body of Christ. If you are born again and filled with the Holy Spirit, you are capable of hearing and following God's voice. John 10:3-4 says, *" . . . the sheep hear his [the Shepherd's] voice; and he calls his own sheep by name and leads them out. And when he brings out his own sheep, he goes before them; and the sheep follow him, for they know his voice."*

God will lead you and confirm His will for your life. Believe me, the Holy Spirit's choice of your spiritual home will be far better for you than any other place you could imagine.

"Those who are <u>planted</u> in the house of the Lord shall flourish in the courts of our God. They shall bear fruit in old age; they shall be fresh and flourishing, to declare that the Lord is upright; He is my rock, and there is no unrighteousness in Him" (Psalm 92:13-15).

Patience also means to be faithful in service and submission to your pastor and local church leadership. The Word of God says to *"obey those who rule over you, and be submissive, for they watch out for your souls, as those who must give account"* (Hebrews 13:17). Some people grow impatient where they have been planted and uproot themselves to pursue their own agendas. Brothers and sisters, this should not be done. If you really believe you have a specific purpose and place in the family of God, you should not look for loopholes to suit your own purposes. Psalm 75:6-7 tells us that promotion comes from the Lord, and Him alone.

I have also seen people leave their local church because they have been offended. They usually end up attending another church, and are shocked when the same thing happens again! Listen to me, jumping from church to church is not God's plan for you. Another church is simply another church. If you know God has *planted* you in your local church, you must ask God to help you work through any problems and allow Him to change your heart. When the Holy Spirit plants you into a body of believers, you are married to the will of God in that place! It is in that church you will achieve your eternal destiny and fulfill a much needed purpose within that body.

Let me give you a paradox. You can be in the work of God, but out of the will of God. This would seem to be impossible, but it happens every day! Jesus said this at the beginning of His ministry, " *'Many will say to me in that day, "Lord, Lord, have we not prophesied in Your name, cast out demons in Your name, and done many wonders in Your name?" And then I will declare to them, "I never knew you: depart from Me, you who practice lawlessness'* " (Matthew 7:22-23). People that attempt to do the works of God outside of His plan of order will face terrible consequences one day.

The local church is your immediate spiritual family within the universal family of God. You cannot abandon your family simply because things do not always go your way! In the Bible, people did not leave their local church; they were "sent" out by the Holy Spirit. In other words, the church leadership confirmed the Spirit's direction for their people and sent them out under the proper spiritual covering (see Acts 13:1-4, 8:14-15, 11:22, 15:27, 17:10, 19:21-22, and Colossians 4:7-8).

What is the bottom line? Let the Holy Spirit plant you in a local church, and be faithful where you are planted!

CONCLUSION
The Final Word

There was once a dynamic local church that underwent a change in leadership. It suffered a time of testing, and in the process, lost many members of its body. Those who remained through the shaking had suffered wounds, but not fatal ones. *You see, this fellowship had been founded on the firm foundation of Jesus Christ and His biblical principles of order.* After dropping to one-third of its original size, this local congregation has now doubled . . . *and is still growing.* God is ordering its functions and making every part of the church body *"beautiful in its time."* The church is now becoming everything God created it to be.

There was once a troubled boy whose heart was broken. He did everything he could think of to fill the void in his heart; things he should not have done. This boy grew into a young man thinking he had to fight to protect his own interests. He hurt other people, trying to put them in their place. Yet, God was patient with him. He replaced his pain and confusion with joy, hope and victory! Today, I am a new man.

God, the creator of the universe and author of the eternal story we call life, has the cameras rolling . . . We each have a script and play an important part in his Master Plan. As we follow God's script and direction, His wisdom guides us. We will move forward *together* and make real progress, instead of running around in endless circles.

God is bringing His people to maturity in these Last Days. He is perfecting His Bride and ordering the functions within the Church to flow *"decently and in order."* Ephesians 4:13-15 says that God is transforming us—

" . . . till we all come to the unity of the faith and of the knowledge of the Son of God, to a perfect man, to the measure of the stature of the fullness of Christ; that we should no longer be children, tossed to and fro and carried about with every wind of doctrine, by the trickery of men, in the cunning craftiness of deceitful plotting, but, speaking the truth in love, may grow up in all things into Him who is the head—Christ . . . "

As Christians humbly submit to the Lord, people everywhere will see the love and unity within the local church and come running into the Light of His presence. *Church, we are being adorned.* We are becoming the glorious Bride that will reign with Christ for eternity. Look in the mirror today, and *see* it by faith! You are royalty. There is a seed of greatness within you.

Be encouraged! It does not matter who you are and what role you play within the local church. If you will wait upon the Lord and trust Him, He will reveal *and* perform His purpose in your life. It will be something that utilizes your greatest talents and fulfills your deepest desires. God has a plan for your life and a special place for you within the local church. *Why don't you take time right now, and search your heart to find the order God has placed within you?*

No matter what challenges you face—the name of Jesus, His power and authority—are greater. His Word and purpose will be fulfilled in your life if you will let patience have its *"perfect work"* in you.

You and I have an appointment with destiny. We must reach out to a lost and dying world, in the strength and power of our Lord, Jesus Christ, and crush the head of the enemy.

OTHER BOOKS AND SPIRITUAL HELPS BY LAWRENCE AND CORAL KENNEDY

ITEM	COST	QUANTITY	TOTAL
—BOOKS—			
1. Rock Foundation	$ 5.50		
2. Supernatural Weapons of Warfare 9.95	~~$ 5.50~~		
3. This Present Victory	$10.00		
4. War in the Heavenlies by Coral Kennedy	$ 9.95		
—AUDIO CASSETTE TAPE SINGLES—			
5. Godly Attitudes Reap Spiritual Altitudes	$ 5.00		
6. Never Let Them See You Faint	$ 5.00		
7. Overcoming Temptation	$ 5.00		
8. The Walls Must Come Down	$ 5.00		
9. Winning Every Time	$ 5.00		
—AUDIO CASSETTE TAPE SERIES—			
10. Be Real	$29.95		
11. Matters of the Heart	$29.95		
12. Power Thinking	$12.95		
13. The Dividing Line	$29.95		
14. Three of My Favorites	$ 9.95		
15. Three of The Top Ten	$ 9.95		
16. Victorious Christian Living	$29.95		
17. War in the Heavenlies by Coral Kennedy	$14.95		
18. Catch The Attitude	$29.95		
19. Last Days in Prophecy	$19.95		
20. Living In The High Places	$19.95		
21. Moving From Level To Level	$34.95		
22. Seven Ingredients of A Champion	$14.95		
23. The Supernatual Anointing of God	$19.95		

TOTAL: $ _____
USA Currency
Shipping & Handling: $ _____
10% USA, 20% Canada
TOTAL ENCLOSED: $ _____

☐CASH ☐CHECK ☐MONEY ORDER CREDIT CARD: ☐VISA ☐MC ☐AMEX

☐☐☐☐☐☐☐☐☐☐☐☐☐☐☐☐

EXPIRATION DATE: ☐☐ - ☐☐ - ☐☐   *Sorry No COD's*

SIGNATURE: _____

Name: _____

Address: _____

City: _____ State: _____ Zip: _____

Phone: (_____) _____

Mail to: Lawrence Kennedy Ministries, 1615 W. Belt Line Road, Carrollton, TX 75006
Fax: 972.245.1978 • Office: 972.242.8989 • WWW.NORTHCHURCH.ORG

***Look for The Upcoming Topics
To Be Addressed in
Dr. Kennedy's Local Church
Government Series!***

Principles of Church Government

Ministry Gifts and Offices

Church Discipline and Unity

Leadership Principles and Practices

Lawrence Kennedy, D.D., Ph.D.

As Pastor of one of the fastest growing churches in America, Dr. Lawrence Kennedy is president of COTR-International Ministries, overseeing 3,100 fellowship churches throughout the nation and around the world. Dr. Kennedy is a powerfully anointed visionary, prophetic teacher, and leader of leaders to the Body of Christ. His singular giftings and deep pastoral burden for God's people have thrust him into national prominence.

Dr. Kennedy has a broad range of ministry experience. He has raised up churches and taught the uncompromising Word of God for more than twenty-seven years. He is also a seasoned author of two books—*Foundations of Order: Understanding The Need for Biblical Church Government in The Last Days*, *This Present Victory*, and two workbooks, *Supernatural Weapons of Warfare*, and *Rock Foundation*. Dr. Kennedy's practical application of Bible truths brings clear direction to God's family.

Dr. Kennedy and his lovely wife, Coral, are founders and senior pastors of The North Church, a congregation in Dallas, Texas that has grown to over 4,000 members in less than nine years. Together they are television co-hosts of *Family & Friends with Lawrence and Coral*.

Having studied in Canada and the United States, Dr. Kennedy earned a Bachelor's degree in Theology, and a Master's Degree in Christian Education. He also holds a Doctor of Divinity from Southern California Theological Seminary and a Doctorate in Christian Psychology from Florida's Jacksonville Theological Seminary.

Prayer / Response Form

❑ I want to learn everything I can about biblical local church government. Please put my name on a list to automatically receive notices of upcoming mini-book volumes in this series.

❑ I am a Christian, but I haven't been *"planted"* in a local church. Please refer me to a church in my area.

❑ Please rush this to Dr. Kennedy's desk for prayer. I need agreement in prayer concerning:

_____

_____

❑ I have just dedicated/re-dedicated my life to Jesus Christ. Please send information to me about how to stay in close fellowship with Him and walk in His Word.

❑ I would like to learn more about the Holy Spirit. Please send information to me about His illuminating ministry in my life.

❑ Please send information to me about the North Church.

❑ Please send information to me about the COTR-International Ministries worldwide network of churches.

Name: _____

Church: _____

Address: _____

_____

Phone: _____

Please provide this information for us . . .

❑ I will be visiting the Dallas/Ft. Worth area.
❑ I am planning a move to the Dallas/Ft. Worth area.
❑ This book has helped me receive victory in my life regarding:

_____

_____